WHY AM I NOT LIVING A VICTORIOUS LIFE?

Prayer Journal

The Keys to Victorious Living Series: Book 4

Charlie O'Neal

Book Cover and Interior Design by: *HFT Publishing, Inc.*

eBook conversion by: *HFT Publishing, Inc.*

HFT PUBLISHING
Inc

HFT Publishing, Inc
P. O. Box 1863
Brewton, AL 36427-1863

Email: HFT-Publishing@post.com

Fax: 251-248-2709

Paperback ISBN: 978-1-735061-3-1
Mobi eBook ISBN: 978-7353061-2-4
ePub eBook ISBN: 978-1-953239-39-6

Printed in the United States of America

DEDICATION

This book is dedicated to all pastors, missionaries, ministers, Christian education teachers, and church leaders that have dedicated their lives to the commission to spread the word of God around the world!

TABLE OF CONTENTS

ACKNOWLEDGMENTS

I want to provide a special "thank you and may God bless you 1000-fold" to all of the Church of God pastors and ministers in the Alabama and Florida areas that helped me with this book, including the editing. I cannot share your names since God has asked that I use a pen name and for no one to receive any rewards or recognition for this book series. But you know, and God knows how much you helped. I pray that he rewards you 1000-fold for your efforts to help get this book into the hands of as many people as possible around the world!

INTRODUCTION

There is a unique story behind the development of this book series. This story is shared in the first book written by Charlie O'Neal. ***Why am I not living a Victorious Life?*** This ministry expansion was initiated by the Director of The Heritage House Foundation after God spoke to her heart. She asked God for confirmation of this ministry expansion before submitting the proposal to the board of directors. Three ministers and two pastors came to her after they had dreams and visions about this ministry, too. Then Charlie O'Neal had a dream with specific instruction for these books and how the royalties would be utilized. This dream was the final confirmation that The Heritage House Foundation needed to begin planning for this expansion.

Now, get out your 90-day devotional and begin studying and writing your prayer request in this journal. Give your schedule and all of your talents to God to utilize. You will learn the Jabez prayer in this study. You will want to memorize it and add it to your daily prayers. Read, study, learn, pray, and watch God bless you!

HOW TO USE THIS PRAYER JOURNAL

This prayer journal was designed to accompany the devotional by the same name. All scriptures utilized in this devotional and prayer journal are taken from the first book of this series, "*Why am I not living a Victorious Life?*" This first devotional and prayer journal includes 90-days of scriptures, thoughts, and devotions. Four (4) devotional and prayer journal sets cover all of the scriptures in this series' first book. The first book is so power-packed that it is hard to give specific "spiritual growth" thoughts to go with each topic and scripture discussed.

Each of these four devotionals will help the reader to take smaller "daily bites" of God's messages to us from this excellent book series. The prayer journal utilizes the same scripture and thought that the devotional covers for that same day. Instead of the devotional content, the prayer journal has a place where you can write down your prayer request, special needs, and answered prayer each day.

To learn more about this author and how these books' profits are donated, read the last two chapters. The ministry that the profits are donated to is covered in the last chapter. For more information on how you can help Heritage House Foundation or learn how this book series was formed, read the book "*Why am I not Living a Victorious Life?*"

One of the greatest tools that Satan uses to keep Christians from praising God, speaking positive words, and declaring victory include Satan stealing from each Christian "memories they need to praise God for each day!" The organization of my life, especially mornings, is a daily challenge at our house. When I began to organize my morning devotional time, I began to see answered prayers. As I noticed an increase in answered prayers, I also noted that my faith was growing—all of this, resulting in a more victorious life.

As a result of this need for organization, I designed a prayer journal to keep you focused on what you need to seek God about and your answered prayers. We are to praise God when our prayers are answered. However, if your day is disorganized and your thoughts scattered because you did not begin your day with God, you will forget to praise God when you kneel to pray at night.

Our Heavenly Father is a God of love. He loves to bless us and meet all of our needs. However, he is a very jealous God. He wants to hear our praises to him daily. He wants to see us put our faith into action! He wants us to love his word (The Bible) so much that we cannot wait to read it each day.

This prayer journal will help you remain focused on your prayer life. As you read the daily devotional, you may want to note things or issues you need to address or pray over. (As I am studying throughout the day, I add to my prayer list for the day). When God moves in your life, or you get a phone call about a miracle or answered prayer, do what I do, immediately document it in your prayer journal.

This may seem like a lot of work, but it is not once you get a routine. This prayer journal saves me time when I am stressed. It keeps me focused, and it keeps me praising God. Our Heavenly Father "inhabits the praises" of his children and longs for this time of communion with us. (KJV, 2020).

The tracking of answered prayer also builds your faith. Satan loves to tell us that our prayers are not answered, that we are wasting our time, or worse, that God does not care! Well, a review of the answered prayers for that week, month, or quarter can send Satan down the road! The more prayers that are answered, the more we praise God for the answered prayers, then the more prayers that God answers for us and the more blessings we receive from our Heavenly Father!

Satan does not like an organized prayer warrior! He despises the fact that we are reminding ourselves of God's blessings and miracles. Satan does not want us to have answered prayers. So, get out your 90-day devotional and begin studying. Write your prayer request in this journal each day. Give your schedule and all of your talents to God to utilize. You will see your life change because of this practice alone. Then you will learn through this study and the reading of the book "*Why am I not Living a Victorious Life*" the essential keys needed to have victory in your home, marriage, and career.

You will also learn the Jabez prayer in this study. I want you to memorize it and incorporate it into your own words into your daily prayers. Read, study, learn, pray, and watch God bless you over these 90 days!

Prayer Journal Day One: _____

_____

I Timothy 1:18-20: This charge I commit unto thee, son Timothy, according to the prophecies which went before on thee, *that thou by them mightest war a good warfare*; holding faith, and a good conscience; which some having put away concerning faith have made shipwreck: Of whom is Hymenaeus and Alexander; whom I have delivered unto Satan, that they may learn not to blaspheme. (KJV, 2020).

_____

Today's Devotional Topic: A Good Warfare Fight

Today's Prayer:

_____
_____
_____
_____
_____
_____
_____
_____
_____
_____
_____
_____
_____
_____
_____

_____
_____
_____
_____
_____

Prayers Answered Today:

_____
_____
_____
_____
_____
_____
_____
_____
_____
_____
_____
_____
_____

Additional Comments:

_____
_____
_____
_____
_____
_____

Prayer Journal Day Two: _____

I Timothy 1:18-20:   This charge I commit unto thee, son Timothy, according to the prophecies which went before on thee, that thou by them mightest war a good warfare; *holding faith*, and a good conscience; which some having put away concerning faith have made shipwreck: Of whom is Hymenaeus and Alexander; whom I have delivered unto Satan, that they may learn not to blaspheme. (KJV, 2020).

Today's Devotional Topic: Holding to your faith

Today's Prayer:

_____

_____

_____

_____

_____

_____

_____

_____

_____

_____

_____

_____

_____

_____

_____

_____

_____

_____

_____

_____

_____

Prayers Answered Today:

_____

_____

_____

_____

_____

_____

_____

_____

_____

_____

_____

Additional Comments:

_____

_____

_____

_____

_____

_____

Prayer Journal Day Three: _____

I Timothy 1:18-20: This charge I commit unto thee, son Timothy, according to the prophecies which went before on thee, that thou by them mightest war a good warfare; Holding faith, and *a good conscience*; which some having put away concerning faith have made shipwreck: Of whom is Hymenaeus and Alexander; whom I have delivered unto Satan, that they may learn not to blaspheme. (KJV, 2020).

Today's Devotional Topic: A Good Conscience

Today's Prayer:

_____

_____

_____

_____

_____

_____

_____

_____

_____

_____

_____

_____

_____

_____

_____

_____

_____
_____
_____
_____
_____

Prayers Answered Today:

_____
_____
_____
_____
_____
_____
_____
_____
_____
_____
_____
_____

Additional Comments:

_____
_____
_____
_____
_____
_____

Prayer Journal Day Four: _____

I Timothy 1:18-20: This charge I commit unto thee, son Timothy, according to the prophecies which went before on thee, that thou by them mightest war a good warfare; Holding faith, and a good conscience; *which some having put away concerning faith have made shipwreck:* Of whom is Hymenaeus and Alexander; whom I have delivered unto Satan, that they may learn not to blaspheme. (KJV, 2020).

Today's Devotional Topic: Lost Faith—The Shipwrecked Life

Today's Prayer:

_____

_____

_____

_____

_____

_____

_____

_____

_____

_____

_____

_____

_____

_____

_____

_____

_____

Prayers Answered Today:

Additional Comments:

Prayer Journal Day Five: _____

Acts 10:4-5:   And when he looked on him, he was afraid, and said, what is it, Lord? And he said unto him, *thy prayers and thine alms are come up for a memorial before God.*   (KJV, 2020).

Today's Devotional Topic: A Memorial Before God

Today's Prayer:

_____

_____

_____

_____

_____

_____

_____

_____

_____

_____

_____

_____

_____

_____

_____

_____

_____

_____

_____

_____

_____

_____

_____

_____

Prayers Answered Today:

_____

_____

_____

_____

_____

_____

_____

_____

_____

_____

_____

_____

Additional Comments:

_____

_____

_____

_____

_____

_____

Prayer Journal Day Six: _____

Proverbs 18:21: Death and life are in *the power of the tongue*: and they that love it shall eat the fruit thereof. (KJV, 2020)

Today's Devotional Topic: The Power of the Tongue

Today's Prayer:

_____

_____

_____

_____

_____

Prayers Answered Today:

_____

_____

_____

_____

_____

_____

_____

_____

_____

_____

_____

_____

Additional Comments:

_____

_____

_____

_____

_____

_____

Prayer Journal Day Seven: _____

Proverbs 18:21: *Death and life* are in the power of the tongue: and they that love it shall eat *the fruit thereof.* (KJV, 2020)

Today's Devotional Topic: Death and Life: The Fruit thereof...

Today's Prayer:

_____

_____

_____

_____

_____

_____

_____

_____

_____

_____

_____

_____

_____

_____

_____

_____

_____

_____

_____

_____

_____

_____

_____

_____

Prayers Answered Today:

_____

_____

_____

_____

_____

_____

_____

_____

_____

_____

_____

Additional Comments:

_____

_____

_____

_____

_____

Prayer Journal Day Eight: _____

Ephesians 4:29-32: *Let no corrupt communication proceed out of your mouth,* but that which is good to the use of edifying, that it may minister grace unto the hearers. And grieve not the holy Spirit of God, whereby ye are sealed unto the day of redemption. Let all bitterness, and wrath, and anger, and clamour, and evil speaking, be put away from you, with all malice: And be ye kind one to another, tenderhearted, forgiving one another, even as God for Christ's sake hath forgiven you. (KJV, 2020).

Today's Devotional Topic: No Corrupt Communication

Today's Prayer:

_____

_____

_____

_____

_____

_____

_____

_____

_____

_____

_____

_____

_____

_____

_____

_____

_____

_____

_____

_____

_____

Prayers Answered Today:

_____

_____

_____

_____

_____

_____

_____

_____

_____

_____

_____

_____

Additional Comments:

_____

_____

_____

_____

_____

_____

Prayer Journal Day Nine: _____

Ephesians 4:29-32: Let no corrupt communication proceed out of your mouth, but that which is good to the use of edifying, that it may minister grace unto the hearers. And *grieve not the Holy Spirit of God, whereby ye are sealed unto the day of redemption.* Let all bitterness, and wrath, and anger, and clamour, and evil speaking, be put away from you, with all malice: And be ye kind one to another, tenderhearted, forgiving one another, even as God for Christ's sake hath forgiven you. (KJV, 2020).

Today's Devotional Topic: Grieve not the Holy Spirit of God.

Today's Prayer:

_____

_____

_____

_____

_____

_____

_____

_____

_____

_____

_____

_____

_____

_____

_____

_____
_____
_____
_____
_____

Prayers Answered Today:

_____
_____
_____
_____
_____
_____
_____
_____
_____
_____
_____
_____

Additional Comments:

_____
_____
_____
_____
_____
_____

Prayer Journal Day Ten: _____

Ephesians 4:29-32: Let no corrupt communication proceed out of your mouth, but that which is good to the use of edifying, that it may minister grace unto the hearers. And grieve not the holy Spirit of God, whereby ye are sealed unto the day of redemption. *Let all bitterness, and wrath, and anger, and clamour, and evil speaking, be put away from you, with all malice.* And be ye kind one to another, tenderhearted, forgiving one another, even as God for Christ's sake hath forgiven you. (KJV, 2020).

Today's Devotional Topic: Bitterness, wrath, anger, clamour, evil speaking, and malice not allowed!

Today's Prayer:

_____
_____
_____
_____
_____
_____
_____
_____
_____
_____
_____
_____
_____
_____
_____

_____

_____

_____

_____

_____

Prayers Answered Today:

_____

_____

_____

_____

_____

_____

_____

_____

_____

_____

_____

Additional Comments:

_____

_____

_____

_____

_____

_____

_____

Prayer Journal Day Eleven: _____

Ephesians 4:29-32: Let no corrupt communication proceed out of your mouth, but that which is good to the use of edifying, that it may minister grace unto the hearers. And grieve not the holy Spirit of God, whereby ye are sealed unto the day of redemption. Let all bitterness, and wrath, and anger, and clamour, and evil speaking, be put away from you, with all malice: *And be ye kind one to another, tenderhearted, forgiving one another, even as God for Christ's sake hath forgiven you.* (KJV, 2020).

Today's Devotional Topic: Tenderhearted with kindness, and forgiving, desired and wanted of all Christians!

Today's Prayer:

_____

_____

_____

_____

_____

_____

_____

_____

_____

_____

_____

_____

_____

_____

_____

_____

_____

_____

_____

_____

Prayers Answered Today:

_____

_____

_____

_____

_____

_____

_____

_____

_____

_____

_____

Additional Comments:

_____

_____

_____

_____

_____

_____

Prayer Journal Day Twelve: _____

I Chronicles 4:9-10: And Jabez was more honourable than his brethren: and his mother called his name Jabez, saying Because I bare him with sorrow. And Jabez called on the God of Israel, saying, *oh, that thou wouldest bless me indeed* and enlarge my coast, and that thine hand might be with me, and that thou wouldest keep *me* from evil, that it may not grieve me! And God granted him that which he requested. (KJV, 2020).

Today's Devotional Topic: Bless me indeed!

Today's Prayer:

_____

_____

_____

_____

_____

_____

_____

_____

_____

_____

_____

_____

_____

_____

_____

_____

_____

_____

_____

_____

_____

Prayers Answered Today:

_____

_____

_____

_____

_____

_____

_____

_____

_____

_____

_____

_____

_____

Additional Comments:

_____

_____

_____

_____

_____

_____

Prayer Journal Day Thirteen: _____

I Chronicles 4:9-10: And Jabez was more honourable than his brethren: and his mother called his name Jabez, saying Because I bare him with sorrow. And Jabez called on the God of Israel, saying, oh, that thou wouldest bless me indeed, and *enlarge my coast, and that thine hand might be with me*, and that thou wouldest keep *me* from evil, that it may not grieve me! And God granted him that which he requested. (KJV, 2020).

Today's Devotional Topic: Enlarge my coast

Today's Prayer:

_____

_____

_____

_____

_____

_____

_____

_____

_____

_____

_____

_____

_____

_____

_____

_____

_____

_____

_____

_____

Prayers Answered Today:

_____

_____

_____

_____

_____

_____

_____

_____

_____

_____

_____

Additional Comments:

_____

_____

_____

_____

_____

_____

_____

Prayer Journal Day Fourteen: _____

I Chronicles 4:9-10: And Jabez was more honourable than his brethren: and his mother called his name Jabez, saying Because I bare him with sorrow. And Jabez called on the God of Israel, saying, oh, that thou wouldest bless me indeed, and enlarge my coast, and that thine hand might be with me, and *that thou wouldest keep me from evil, that it may not grieve me!* And God granted him that which he requested. (KJV, 2020).

Today's Devotional Topic: God, please keep us from evil!

Today's Prayer:

_____

_____

_____

_____

_____

_____

_____

_____

_____

_____

_____

_____

_____

_____

_____

_____

_____

_____

_____

_____

Prayers Answered Today:

_____

_____

_____

_____

_____

_____

_____

_____

_____

_____

_____

_____

Additional Comments:

_____

_____

_____

_____

_____

Prayer Journal Day Fifteen: _____

Psalm 55:22: Cast thy burden upon the LORD, and he shall sustain thee: he shall never suffer the righteous to be moved. (KJV, 2020).

Today's Devotional Topic: Cast Your Burdens on Jesus

Today's Prayer:

_____

_____

_____

_____

_____

_____

_____

_____

_____

_____

_____

_____

_____

_____

_____

_____

_____

_____

_____

_____

_____

_____

_____

_____

Prayers Answered Today:

_____

_____

_____

_____

_____

_____

_____

_____

_____

_____

_____

Additional Comments:

_____

_____

_____

_____

_____

_____

Prayer Journal Day Sixteen: _____

I Peter 5:6-7: Humble yourselves therefore under the mighty hand of God that he may exalt you in due time: Casting all your care upon him; for he careth for you. (KJV, 2020).

Today's Devotional Topic: Humble yourself before God.

Today's Prayer:

_____

_____

_____

_____

_____

_____

_____

_____

_____

_____

_____

_____

_____

_____

_____

_____

_____

_____

_____

_____

_____

_____

_____

_____

Prayers Answered Today:

_____

_____

_____

_____

_____

_____

_____

_____

_____

_____

_____

_____

Additional Comments:

_____

_____

_____

_____

_____

_____

Prayer Journal Day Seventeen: _____

Matthew 16:19: And I will give unto thee the keys of the kingdom of heaven: and whatsoever thou shalt bind on earth shall be bound in heaven: and whatsoever thou shalt loose on earth shall be loosed in heaven. (KJV, 2020).

Today's Devotional Topic: Keys to the Kingdom

Today's Prayer:

_____

_____

_____

_____

_____

_____

_____

_____

_____

_____

_____

_____

_____

_____

_____

_____

_____

_____

_____
_____
_____
_____
_____

Prayers Answered Today:

_____
_____
_____
_____
_____
_____
_____
_____
_____
_____
_____
_____

Additional Comments:

_____
_____
_____
_____
_____
_____
_____

Prayer Journal Day Eighteen: _____

Matthew 16:19: And I will give unto thee the keys of the kingdom of heaven: and whatsoever thou shalt bind on earth shall be bound in heaven: and whatsoever thou shalt loose on earth shall be loosed in heaven. (KJV, 2020).

Today's Devotional Topic: Spiritually binding things here on earth

Today's Prayer:

_____

_____

_____

_____

_____

_____

_____

_____

_____

_____

_____

_____

_____

_____

_____

_____

_____

_____

_____
_____
_____
_____
_____

Prayers Answered Today:

_____
_____
_____
_____
_____
_____
_____
_____
_____
_____
_____
_____
_____

Additional Comments:

_____
_____
_____
_____
_____
_____
_____

Prayer Journal Day Nineteen: _____

Psalm 139:7-10: Whither shall I go from thy spirit? Or whither shall I flee from thy presence? If I ascend into heaven, thou art there: if I make my bed in hell, behold, thou art there. If I take the wings of the morning and dwell in the uttermost parts of the sea; Even there shall thy hand lead me, and thy right hand shall hold me. (KJV, 2020).

Today's Devotional Topic: Anywhere to hide?

Today's Prayer:

_____

_____

_____

_____

_____

_____

_____

_____

_____

_____

_____

_____

_____

_____

_____

_____

_____

_____

_____

_____

_____

_____

_____

Prayers Answered Today:

_____

_____

_____

_____

_____

_____

_____

_____

_____

_____

_____

_____

Additional Comments:

_____

_____

_____

_____

_____

Prayer Journal Day Twenty: _____

Psalm 119:33-34: *Teach me, O LORD, the way of thy statutes;* and I shall keep it unto the end. Give me understanding, and I shall keep thy law; yea, I shall observe it with my whole heart. (KJV, 2020).

Today's Devotional Topic: Teach me, Oh, Lord, how you want me to live and what you want me to do!

Today's Prayer:

_____

_____

_____

_____

_____

_____

_____

_____

_____

_____

_____

_____

_____

_____

_____

_____

_____

_____

_____

_____

_____

_____

_____

Prayers Answered Today:

_____

_____

_____

_____

_____

_____

_____

_____

_____

_____

_____

Additional Comments:

_____

_____

_____

_____

_____

Prayer Journal Day Twenty-One: _____

Psalm 119:33-34: Teach me, O LORD, the way of thy statutes; and I shall keep it unto the end. *Give me understanding, and I shall keep thy law; yea, I shall observe it with my whole heart.* (KJV, 2020).

Today's Devotional Topic: We need anointing to understand God's word and keep his commandments with our whole heart!

Today's Prayer:

_____
_____
_____
_____
_____
_____
_____
_____
_____
_____
_____
_____
_____
_____
_____
_____
_____
_____

_____

_____

_____

_____

_____

Prayers Answered Today:

_____

_____

_____

_____

_____

_____

_____

_____

_____

_____

Additional Comments:

_____

_____

_____

_____

_____

_____

_____

Prayer Journal Day Twenty-Two: _____

Leviticus 20:8: And ye shall keep my statutes, and do them: I *am* the LORD which sanctify you. (KJV, 2020).

Deuteronomy 11:22:
For if ye shall diligently keep all these commandments which I command you, to do them, to love the LORD your God, to walk in all his ways, and to cleave unto him;

Today's Devotional Topic: A Good Walk—keeping God's commandments and cleaving to the Lord, who will sanctify us for his glory! Amen!

Today's Prayer:

_____

_____

_____

_____

_____

_____

_____

_____

_____

_____

_____

_____

_____

_____

_____

_____

_____

_____

_____

_____

Prayers Answered Today:

_____

_____

_____

_____

_____

_____

_____

_____

_____

_____

_____

_____

Additional Comments:

_____

_____

_____

_____

_____

_____

Prayer Journal Day Twenty-Three: _____

John 8:51: Verily, verily, I say unto you, if a man keeps my saying, he shall never see death. (KJV, 2020).

Today's Devotional Topic: Is it possible that we could never die?

Today's Prayer:

_____
_____
_____
_____
_____
_____
_____
_____
_____
_____
_____
_____
_____
_____
_____
_____
_____
_____

_____
_____
_____
_____
_____

Prayers Answered Today:

_____
_____
_____
_____
_____
_____
_____
_____
_____
_____
_____
_____
_____

Additional Comments:

_____
_____
_____
_____
_____

Prayer Journal Day Twenty-Four: _____

II Thessalonians 3:3: But the Lord is faithful, who shall establish you, and keep *you* from evil. (KJV, 2020).

Today's Devotional Topic: Lord, please keep us from evil!

Today's Prayer:

_____

_____

_____

_____

_____

Prayers Answered Today:

_____

_____

_____

_____

_____

_____

_____

_____

_____

_____

_____

Additional Comments:

_____

_____

_____

_____

_____

_____

Prayer Journal Day Twenty-Five: _____

Jude 1:24: Now unto him, that is able to keep you from falling and to present you faultless before the presence of his glory with exceeding joy. (KJV, 2020).

Today's Devotional Topic: God can keep us!

Today's Prayer:

_____

_____

_____

_____

_____

_____

_____

_____

_____

_____

_____

_____

_____

_____

_____

_____

_____

_____

_____

_____

_____

_____

_____

_____

Prayers Answered Today:

_____

_____

_____

_____

_____

_____

_____

_____

_____

_____

_____

Additional Comments:

_____

_____

_____

_____

_____

_____

Prayer Journal Day Twenty-Six: _____

John 11:35: Jesus Wept! (KJV, 2020).

Today's Devotional Topic: A Good Cry!

Today's Prayer:

_____

_____

_____

_____

_____

Prayers Answered Today:

_____

_____

_____

_____

_____

_____

_____

_____

_____

_____

_____

_____

Additional Comments:

_____

_____

_____

_____

_____

Prayer Journal Day Twenty-Seven: _____

John 3:16-17: *For God so loved the world that he gave his only begotten son, that whosoever believed on him might be saved.* He sent not his Son into the world to condemn the world, but that through him they might be saved. (KJV, 2020).

Today's Devotional Topic: Grace and Mercy

Today's Prayer:

_____

_____

_____

_____

_____

Prayers Answered Today:

_____

_____

_____

_____

_____

_____

_____

_____

_____

_____

_____

Additional Comments:

_____

_____

_____

_____

_____

_____

Prayer Journal Day Twenty-Eight: _____

John 3:16-17: For God so loved the world that he gave his only begotten son, that whosoever believed on him might be saved. *He sent not his Son into the world to condemn the world, but that through him they might be saved.* (KJV, 2020).

Today's Devotional Topic: No Condemnation Allowed

Today's Prayer:

_____

_____

_____

_____

_____

_____

_____

_____

_____

_____

_____

_____

_____

_____

_____

_____

_____

_____

_____

_____

_____

_____

_____

Prayers Answered Today:

_____

_____

_____

_____

_____

_____

_____

_____

_____

_____

_____

Additional Comments:

_____

_____

_____

_____

_____

_____

Prayer Journal Day Twenty-Nine: _____

II Peter 2:9: The Lord knoweth how to deliver the godly out of temptations, and to reserve the unjust unto the day of judgment to be punished: (KJV, 2020).

Today's Devotional Topic: Deliverance from Temptation

Today's Prayer:

_____

_____

_____

_____

_____

_____

_____

_____

_____

_____

_____

_____

_____

_____

_____

_____

_____

_____

_____

_____

_____
_____
_____
_____
_____

Prayers Answered Today:

_____
_____
_____
_____
_____
_____
_____
_____
_____
_____
_____
_____
_____

Additional Comments:

_____
_____
_____
_____
_____
_____

Prayer Journal Day Thirty: _____

II Timothy 1:12: For the which cause I also suffer these things: nevertheless, I am not ashamed: for I know whom I have believed, and am persuaded that he is able to keep that which I have committed unto him against that day. (KJV, 2020).

Today's Devotional Topic: God's Awesome Grace

Today's Prayer:

_____
_____
_____
_____
_____

Prayers Answered Today:

_____
_____
_____
_____
_____
_____
_____
_____
_____
_____
_____
_____

Additional Comments:

_____
_____
_____
_____
_____
_____

Prayer Journal Day Thirty-One: _____

Isaiah 26:3-4: Thou wilt keep him in perfect peace, whose mind is stayed on thee: because he trusteth in thee. Trust ye in the LORD forever: for in the LORD JEHOVAH is everlasting strength: (JKV, 2019).

Today's Devotional Topic: Perfect peace, trust, and everlasting strength through Jesus Christ

Today's Prayer:

_____

_____

_____

_____

_____

_____

_____

_____

_____

_____

_____

_____

_____

_____

_____

_____

_____

_____

_____

_____

_____

_____

_____

_____

Prayers Answered Today:

_____

_____

_____

_____

_____

_____

_____

_____

_____

_____

Additional Comments:

_____

_____

_____

_____

_____

_____

Prayer Journal Thirty-Two: _____

Malachi 3:11: And I will rebuke the devourer for your sakes, and he shall not destroy the fruits of your ground; neither shall your vine cast her fruit before the time in the field, saith the LORD of hosts. (KJV, 2020).

Today's Devotional Topic: He rebukes the devourer for our sakes!

Today's Prayer:

_____

_____

_____

_____

_____

_____

_____

_____

_____

_____

_____

_____

_____

_____

_____

_____

_____

_____

_____

_____

_____

_____

_____

Prayers Answered Today:

_____

_____

_____

_____

_____

_____

_____

_____

_____

_____

_____

Additional Comments:

_____

_____

_____

_____

_____

Prayer Journal Day Thirty-Three: _____

Psalm 139:23-24: *Search me, O God, and know my heart*: try me, and know my thoughts: And see if there be any wicked way in me, and lead me in the way everlasting. (KJV, 2020).

Today's Devotional Topic: Know my heart, Oh God!

Today's Prayer:

_____

_____

_____

_____

_____

_____

_____

_____

_____

_____

_____

_____

_____

_____

_____

_____

_____

_____

_____

_____

_____

_____

_____

_____

Prayers Answered Today:

_____

_____

_____

_____

_____

_____

_____

_____

_____

_____

_____

_____

Additional Comments:

_____

_____

_____

_____

_____

Prayer Journal Day Thirty-Four: _____

Psalm 139:23-24: Search me, O God, and know my heart: *try me, and know my thoughts: And see if there be any wicked way in me,* and lead me in the way everlasting. (KJV, 2020).

Today's Devotional Topic: Try me, know my thoughts-remove all evil from my life!

Today's Prayer:

_____

_____

_____

_____

_____

_____

_____

_____

_____

_____

_____

_____

_____

_____

_____

_____

_____

_____

_____

_____

_____

_____

_____

_____

Prayers Answered Today:

_____

_____

_____

_____

_____

_____

_____

_____

_____

_____

_____

Additional Comments:

_____

_____

_____

_____

_____

Prayer Journal Day Thirty-Five: _____

Psalm 139:23-24: Search me, O God, and know my heart: try me, and know my thoughts: And see if there be any wicked way in me, and *lead me in the way everlasting*. (KJV, 2020).

<u>Today's Devotional Topic</u>: Lead me, Lord, to my purpose!

<u>Today's Prayer:</u>

_____

_____

_____

_____

_____

_____

_____

_____

_____

_____

_____

_____

_____

_____

_____

_____

_____

_____
_____
_____
_____
_____

Prayers Answered Today:

_____
_____
_____
_____
_____
_____
_____
_____
_____
_____
_____
_____
_____

Additional Comments:

_____
_____
_____
_____
_____
_____
_____

Prayer Journal Day Thirty-Six: _____

Job 22:28: Thou shalt also decree a thing, and it shall be established unto thee: and the light shall shine upon thy ways. (KJV, 2020).

Today's Devotional Topic: Declare it in the name of the Lord, so it shall be established.

Today's Prayer:

_____

_____

_____

_____

_____

_____

_____

_____

_____

_____

_____

_____

_____

_____

_____

_____

_____

_____

_____

_____

_____

_____

_____

Prayers Answered Today:

_____

_____

_____

_____

_____

_____

_____

_____

_____

_____

_____

_____

Additional Comments:

_____

_____

_____

_____

_____

_____

Prayer Journal Day Thirty-Seven: _____

II Timothy 1:12: For the which cause I also suffer these things: nevertheless, I am not ashamed: for I know whom I have believed, and am persuaded that he is able to keep that which I have committed unto him against that day. (KJV, 2020).

Today's Devotional Topic: I am persuaded in who I believe

Today's Prayer:

_____

_____

_____

_____

_____

_____

_____

_____

_____

_____

_____

_____

_____

_____

_____

_____

_____

_____

_____

_____

_____

_____

_____

Prayers Answered Today:

_____

_____

_____

_____

_____

_____

_____

_____

_____

_____

_____

_____

Additional Comments:

_____

_____

_____

_____

_____

Prayer Journal Day Thirty-Eight: _____

Isaiah 26:3-4: Thou wilt keep *him* in perfect peace, *whose* mind *is* stayed *on thee*: because he trusteth in thee. Trust ye in the LORD forever: for in the LORD JEHOVAH *is* everlasting strength: (KJV, 2020).

Today's Devotional Topic: Trust in the Lord...he will keep you!

Today's Prayer:

_____

_____

_____

_____

_____

_____

_____

_____

_____

_____

_____

_____

_____

_____

_____

_____

_____

_____

_____

_____

_____

_____

_____

Prayers Answered Today:

_____

_____

_____

_____

_____

_____

_____

_____

_____

_____

_____

Additional Comments:

_____

_____

_____

_____

_____

_____

Prayer Journal Day Thirty-Nine: _____

III John 1:2: Beloved, I pray that you may prosper in all things and be in health, just as your soul prospers. (KJV, 2020).

Today's Devotional Topic: God wants you to prosper and be healthy!

Today's Prayer:

_____

_____

_____

_____

_____

Prayers Answered Today:

_____

_____

_____

_____

_____

_____

_____

_____

_____

_____

_____

Additional Comments:

_____

_____

_____

_____

_____

_____

Prayer Journal Day Forty: _____

Job 22:28: Thou shalt also decree a thing, and it shall be established unto thee: and the light shall shine upon thy ways. (KJV, 2020).

Today's Devotional Topic: Decree it and watch God establish it!

Today's Prayer:

_____

_____

_____

_____

_____

_____

_____

_____

_____

_____

_____

_____

_____

_____

_____

_____

_____

_____

_____

_____

_____

_____

_____

_____

Prayers Answered Today:

_____

_____

_____

_____

_____

_____

_____

_____

_____

_____

_____

Additional Comments:

_____

_____

_____

_____

_____

Prayer Journal Day Forty-One: _____

Colossians 1:13: Who hath delivered us from the power of darkness, and hath translated *us* into the kingdom of his dear Son: (JKV, 2019).

Today's Devotional Topic: Thanks for deliverance from darkness!

Today's Prayer:

_____

_____

_____

_____

_____

_____

_____

_____

_____

_____

_____

_____

_____

_____

_____

_____

_____

_____

_____

_____

_____
_____
_____
_____
_____

Prayers Answered Today:

_____
_____
_____
_____
_____
_____
_____
_____
_____
_____
_____
_____
_____

Additional Comments:

_____
_____
_____
_____
_____
_____

Prayer Journal Day Forty-Two: _____

Galatians 2:20: *I am crucified with Christ*: nevertheless, I live; yet not I, but Christ liveth in me: and the life which I now live in the flesh I live by the faith of the Son of God, who loved me and gave himself for me. (JKV, 2019).

Today's Devotional Topic: I am crucified with Christ!

Today's Prayer:

_____

_____

_____

_____

_____

_____

_____

_____

_____

_____

_____

_____

_____

_____

_____

_____

_____

_____

_____

_____

_____

_____

_____

Prayers Answered Today:

_____

_____

_____

_____

_____

_____

_____

_____

_____

_____

_____

_____

Additional Comments:

_____

_____

_____

_____

_____

Prayer Journal Day Forty-Three: _____

Galatians 2:20: I am crucified with Christ: *nevertheless, I live; yet not I, but Christ liveth in me:* and the life which I now live in the flesh I live by the faith of the Son of God, who loved me and gave himself for me. (JKV, 2019).

Today's Devotional Topic: Christ Lives in Me, Amen!

Today's Prayer:

_____

_____

_____

_____

_____

_____

_____

_____

_____

_____

_____

_____

_____

_____

_____

_____

_____

_____

_____

_____

_____

_____

_____

_____

Prayers Answered Today:

_____

_____

_____

_____

_____

_____

_____

_____

_____

_____

_____

_____

Additional Comments:

_____

_____

_____

_____

_____

Prayer Journal Day Forty-Four: _____

Galatians 2:20: I am crucified with Christ: nevertheless, I live; yet not I, but Christ liveth in me: and the life which I now live in the flesh *I live by the faith of the Son of God, who loved me and gave himself for me.* (JKV, 2019).

Today's Devotional Topic: I live by Faith!

Today's Prayer:

_____

_____

_____

_____

_____

_____

_____

_____

_____

_____

_____

_____

_____

_____

_____

_____

_____

_____

_____

_____

_____

_____

_____

_____

Prayers Answered Today:

_____

_____

_____

_____

_____

_____

_____

_____

_____

_____

_____

_____

Additional Comments:

_____

_____

_____

_____

_____

Prayer Journal Day Forty-Five: _____

Romans 6:4-5: We are buried with Him [Jesus] through baptism into death, that just as Christ was raised from the dead by the glory of the Father, even so, we also should walk in newness of life. (KJV, 2020)

Today's Devotional Topic: Buried in Christ...walking in a new life!

Today's Prayer:

_____

_____

_____

_____

_____

_____

_____

_____

_____

_____

_____

_____

_____

_____

_____

_____

_____

_____

_____
_____
_____
_____
_____

Prayers Answered Today:

_____
_____
_____
_____
_____
_____
_____
_____
_____
_____
_____
_____

Additional Comments:

_____
_____
_____
_____
_____

Prayer Journal Day Forty-Six: _____

Romans 13:11-12: And that, knowing the time, that now *it is* high time to awake out of sleep: for now, *is* our salvation nearer than when we believed. The night is far spent, the day is at hand: let us, therefore, cast off the works of darkness and let us put on the armour of light. (KJV, 2020).

Today's Devotional Topic: Our Salvation is nearer than we believe!

Today's Prayer:

_____

_____

_____

_____

_____

_____

_____

_____

_____

_____

_____

_____

_____

_____

_____

_____

_____

_____

_____

_____

_____

_____

_____

Prayers Answered Today:

_____

_____

_____

_____

_____

_____

_____

_____

_____

_____

_____

_____

Additional Comments:

_____

_____

_____

_____

_____

Prayer Journal Day Forty-Seven: _____

Galatians 5:22-23: But the *fruit of the Spirit* is *love,* joy, peace, longsuffering, gentleness, goodness, faith, meekness, temperance: against such; there is no law. (KJV, 2020).

Today's Devotional Topic: **Love:** Christ's love and the love we need to give to others!

Today's Prayer:

_____

_____

_____

_____

_____

_____

_____

_____

_____

_____

_____

_____

_____

_____

_____

_____

_____

_____

_____

_____

_____

_____

_____

Prayers Answered Today:

_____

_____

_____

_____

_____

_____

_____

_____

_____

_____

_____

Additional Comments:

_____

_____

_____

_____

_____

Prayer Journal Day Forty-Eight: _____

Galatians 5:22-23: But the *fruit of the Spirit* is love, *joy*, peace, longsuffering, gentleness, goodness, faith, meekness, temperance: against such; there is no law. (KJV, 2020).

Today's Devotional Topic: Joy: Sharing the Joy of our Salvation

Today's Prayer:

_____

_____

_____

_____

_____

_____

_____

_____

_____

_____

_____

_____

_____

_____

_____

_____

_____

_____

_____

_____

_____

_____

_____

Prayers Answered Today:

_____

_____

_____

_____

_____

_____

_____

_____

_____

_____

_____

_____

Additional Comments:

_____

_____

_____

_____

_____

Prayer Journal Day Forty-Nine: _____

Galatians 5:22-23: But the *fruit of the Spirit* is love, joy, ***peace,*** longsuffering, gentleness, goodness, faith, meekness, temperance: against such; there is no law. (KJV, 2020).

Today's Devotional Topic: **Peace:** Only God can give this type of Peace

Today's Prayer:

_____

_____

_____

_____

_____

_____

_____

_____

_____

_____

_____

_____

_____

_____

_____

_____

_____

_____

_____

_____

_____

_____

_____

_____

Prayers Answered Today:

_____

_____

_____

_____

_____

_____

_____

_____

_____

_____

_____

_____

Additional Comments:

_____

_____

_____

_____

_____

_____

Prayer Journal Day Fifty: _____

Galatians 5:22-23: But the *fruit of the Spirit* is love, joy, peace, *longsuffering*, gentleness, goodness, faith, meekness, temperance: against such; there is no law. (KJV, 2020).

Today's Devotional Topic: The Challenges of being Longsuffering

Today's Prayer:

_____

_____

_____

_____

_____

_____

_____

_____

_____

_____

_____

_____

_____

_____

_____

_____

_____

_____

_____
_____
_____
_____
_____

Prayers Answered Today:

_____
_____
_____
_____
_____
_____
_____
_____
_____
_____
_____
_____

Additional Comments:

_____
_____
_____
_____
_____

Prayer Journal Day Fifty-One: _____

Galatians 5:22-23: But the *fruit of the Spirit* is love, joy, peace, longsuffering, **gentleness**, goodness, faith, meekness, temperance: against such; there is no law. (KJV, 2020).

Today's Devotional Topic: Gentleness is a special gift from our Father!

Today's Prayer:

_____

_____

_____

_____

_____

_____

_____

_____

_____

_____

_____

_____

_____

_____

_____

_____

_____

_____

_____

_____

_____

_____

_____

_____

_____

Prayers Answered Today:

_____

_____

_____

_____

_____

_____

_____

_____

_____

_____

_____

Additional Comments:

_____

_____

_____

_____

_____

Prayer Journal Day Fifty-Two: _____

Galatians 5:22-23: But the *fruit of the Spirit* is love, joy, peace, longsuffering, gentleness, *goodnes*s, faith, meekness, temperance: against such; there is no law. (KJV, 2020).

Today's Devotional Topic: Goodness is a witness to your new heart!

Today's Prayer:

_____

_____

_____

_____

_____

_____

_____

_____

_____

_____

_____

_____

_____

_____

_____

_____

_____

_____

_____

_____

_____

_____

_____

Prayers Answered Today:

_____

_____

_____

_____

_____

_____

_____

_____

_____

_____

_____

Additional Comments:

_____

_____

_____

_____

_____

Prayer Journal Day Fifty-Three: _____

Galatians 5:22-23: But the *fruit of the Spirit* is love, joy, peace, longsuffering, gentleness, goodness, *faith*, meekness, temperance: against such; there is no law. (KJV, 2020).

Today's Devotional Topic: A faith that works!

Today's Prayer:

_____

_____

_____

_____

_____

_____

_____

_____

_____

_____

_____

_____

_____

_____

_____

_____

_____

_____

_____

_____

_____

_____

_____

Prayers Answered Today:

_____

_____

_____

_____

_____

_____

_____

_____

_____

_____

_____

_____

Additional Comments:

_____

_____

_____

_____

_____

Prayer Journal Day Fifty-Four: _____

Galatians 5:22-23: But the *fruit of the Spirit* is love, joy, peace, longsuffering, gentleness, goodness, faith, **_meekness_**, temperance: against such; there is no law. (KJV, 2020).

Today's Devotional Topic: Meekness without struggling.

Today's Prayer:

_____

_____

_____

_____

_____

_____

_____

_____

_____

_____

_____

_____

_____

_____

_____

_____

_____

_____

_____

_____

_____

_____

_____

Prayers Answered Today:

_____

_____

_____

_____

_____

_____

_____

_____

_____

_____

_____

_____

Additional Comments:

_____

_____

_____

_____

_____

Prayer Journal Day Fifty-Five: _____

Galatians 5:22-23: But the *fruit of the Spirit* is love, joy, peace, longsuffering, gentleness, goodness, faith, meekness, *temperance*: against such; there is no law. (KJV, 2020).

Today's Devotional Topic: Temperance in all things.

Today's Prayer:

_____

_____

_____

_____

_____

_____

_____

_____

_____

_____

_____

_____

_____

_____

_____

_____

_____

_____

_____

_____

_____

_____

_____

_____

Prayers Answered Today:

_____

_____

_____

_____

_____

_____

_____

_____

_____

_____

_____

_____

Additional Comments:

_____

_____

_____

_____

_____

_____

Prayer Journal Day Fifty-Six: _____

I John 4:4: Ye are of God, little children, and have overcome them: because greater is he that is in you than he that is in the world. (KJV, 2020).

Today's Devotional Topic: With the Holy Spirit living in us, we are equipped to handle anything that this world and Satan sends our way this year!

Today's Prayer:

_____
_____
_____
_____
_____
_____
_____
_____
_____
_____
_____
_____
_____
_____
_____
_____
_____
_____
_____

_____

_____

_____

_____

_____

Prayers Answered Today:

_____

_____

_____

_____

_____

_____

_____

_____

_____

_____

_____

_____

Additional Comments:

_____

_____

_____

_____

_____

Prayer Journal Day Fifty-Seven: _____

Luke 4:1-2: And Jesus being full of the Holy Ghost returned from Jordan and was *led by the Spirit into the wilderness, being forty days tempted of the devil. And in those days, he did eat nothing*: and when they were ended, he afterward hungered. (KJV, 2020).

Today's Devotional Topic: Separate yourself, fast, and pray often.

Today's Prayer:

_____

_____

_____

_____

_____

_____

_____

_____

_____

_____

_____

_____

_____

_____

_____

_____

_____

_____
_____
_____
_____
_____

Prayers Answered Today:

_____
_____
_____
_____
_____
_____
_____
_____
_____
_____
_____
_____
_____

Additional Comments:

_____
_____
_____
_____
_____

Prayer Journal Day Fifty-Eight: _____

Luke 4:2: Being forty days tempted of the devil. And in those days, he *[Jesus] did eat nothing*: and when they were ended, he afterward hungered. (KJV, 2020).

Today's Devotional Topic: Following Jesus' example--Fasting for power

Today's Prayer:

_____

_____

_____

_____

_____

_____

_____

_____

_____

_____

_____

_____

_____

_____

_____

_____

_____

_____

_____

_____
_____
_____
_____
_____

Prayers Answered Today:

_____
_____
_____
_____
_____
_____
_____
_____
_____
_____
_____
_____

Additional Comments:

_____
_____
_____
_____
_____

Prayer Journal Day Fifty-Nine: _____

Luke 4:3-4: And the devil said unto him [Jesus], If thou be the Son of God, command this stone that it be made bread. And Jesus answered him, saying, it is written, that man shall not live by bread alone, but by every word of God. (KJV, 2020).

Today's Devotional Topic: We live not by bread but by the word of God! Quote the word to Satan to obtain your victory!

Today's Prayer:

_____

_____

_____

_____

_____

_____

_____

_____

_____

_____

_____

_____

_____

_____

_____

_____

_____

_____

_____

_____

_____

_____

_____

_____

Prayers Answered Today:

_____

_____

_____

_____

_____

_____

_____

_____

_____

_____

Additional Comments:

_____

_____

_____

_____

_____

Prayer Journal Day Sixty: _____

Luke 4:4: And Jesus answered him saying, it is written, that man shall not live by bread alone, but by every word of God. (KJV, 2020).

Today's Devotional Topic: We need the word of God (the Bible) in our lives each day so that we can grow spiritually and succeed in the battlefield of our minds!

Today's Prayer:

_____

_____

_____

_____

_____

_____

_____

_____

_____

_____

_____

_____

_____

_____

_____

_____

_____

_____

_____

_____

_____

_____

_____

Prayers Answered Today:

_____

_____

_____

_____

_____

_____

_____

_____

_____

_____

_____

Additional Comments:

_____

_____

_____

_____

_____

Prayer Journal Day Sixty-One: _____

Luke 4:8: And Jesus answered and said unto him, get thee behind me, Satan: for it is written, thou shalt worship the Lord thy God, and him only shalt thou serve. (KJV, 2020).

Today's Devotional Topic: Serve the Lord and worship him with all of your heart! Even Satan will have to bow down and worship God soon.

Today's Prayer:

_____

_____

_____

_____

_____

_____

_____

_____

_____

_____

_____

_____

_____

_____

_____

_____

_____

_____

_____
_____
_____
_____
_____

Prayers Answered Today:

_____
_____
_____
_____
_____
_____
_____
_____
_____
_____
_____
_____

Additional Comments:

_____
_____
_____
_____
_____
_____

Prayer Journal Day Sixty-Two: _____

Luke 4:9-13: And he brought him to Jerusalem, and set him on a pinnacle of the temple, and said unto him, if thou be the Son of God, cast thyself down from hence: For it is written, He shall give his angels charge over thee, to keep thee: And in their hands, they shall bear thee up, lest at any time thou dash thy foot against a stone. And Jesus answering said unto him, it is said, thou shalt not tempt the Lord thy God. And when the devil had ended all the temptation, he departed from him for a season. (KJV, 2020).

Today's Devotional Topic: Stand and know Jesus is Lord in our lives, and he always wins in the end!

Today's Prayer:

_____

_____

_____

_____

_____

_____

_____

_____

_____

_____

_____

_____

_____

Prayers Answered Today:

Additional Comments:

Prayer Journal Day Sixty-Three: _____

Galatians 6:7: Be not deceived; God is not mocked: for whatsoever a man soweth, that shall he also reap. (KJV, 2020).

Today's Devotional Topic: We reap what we sow…plant good seeds!

Today's Prayer:

_____

_____

_____

_____

_____

_____

_____

_____

_____

_____

_____

_____

_____

_____

_____

_____

_____

_____

_____

_____

_____

_____

_____

_____

Prayers Answered Today:

_____

_____

_____

_____

_____

_____

_____

_____

_____

_____

_____

Additional Comments:

_____

_____

_____

_____

_____

Prayer Journal Day Sixty-Four: _____

Jeremiah 1:12: Then said the LORD unto me, thou hast well seen: for I will hasten my word to perform it. (KJV, 2020).

Today's Devotional Topic: God will hasten to perform a good work in us and bless us!

Today's Prayer:

_____
_____
_____
_____
_____
_____
_____
_____
_____
_____
_____
_____
_____
_____
_____
_____
_____
_____
_____

_____

_____

_____

_____

_____

_____

Prayers Answered Today:

_____

_____

_____

_____

_____

_____

_____

_____

_____

_____

_____

Additional Comments:

_____

_____

_____

_____

_____

Prayer Journal Day Sixty-Five: _____

Revelation 1:18: I am he that liveth, and was dead; and, behold, I am alive forevermore, amen; and have the keys of hell and of death. (KJV, 2020).

Today's Devotional Topic: God controls life and death and holds the keys to hell and death.

Today's Prayer:

_____
_____
_____
_____
_____
_____
_____
_____
_____
_____
_____
_____
_____
_____
_____
_____
_____
_____

_____
_____
_____
_____
_____

Prayers Answered Today:

_____
_____
_____
_____
_____
_____
_____
_____
_____
_____
_____
_____

Additional Comments:

_____
_____
_____
_____
_____

Prayer Journal Day Sixty-Six: _____

Galatians 5:14: Thou shalt love thy neighbor as thyself. (KJV, 2020).

Today's Devotional Topic: The greatest commandment for the Christian believer is to love, forgive, and forget!

Today's Prayer:

_____

_____

_____

_____

_____

_____

_____

_____

_____

_____

_____

_____

_____

_____

_____

_____

_____

_____

_____

_____

_____

_____

_____

_____

_____

Prayers Answered Today:

_____

_____

_____

_____

_____

_____

_____

_____

_____

_____

_____

Additional Comments:

_____

_____

_____

_____

_____

Prayer Journal Day Sixty-Seven: _____

Hebrews 11:6: *But without faith, it is impossible to please him:* for he that cometh to God must believe that He is and that He is a rewarder of them that diligently seek him (KJV, 2020).

Today's Devotional Topic: It is impossible to please God without faith!

Today's Prayer:

_____

_____

_____

_____

_____

_____

_____

_____

_____

_____

_____

_____

_____

_____

_____

_____

_____

_____

_____

_____

_____

_____

_____

_____

Prayers Answered Today:

_____

_____

_____

_____

_____

_____

_____

_____

_____

_____

_____

Additional Comments:

_____

_____

_____

_____

_____

Prayer Journal Day Sixty-Eight: _____

Hebrews 11:6: But without faith, it is impossible to please him: for he that cometh to God must believe that He is and that *He is a rewarder of them that diligently seek him.* (KJV, 2020).

Today's Devotional Topic: Diligently seek the Lord!

Today's Prayer:

_____

_____

_____

_____

_____

_____

_____

_____

_____

_____

_____

_____

_____

_____

_____

_____

_____

_____

Prayers Answered Today:

Additional Comments:

Prayer Journal Day Sixty-Nine: _____

Galatians 5:1: *Stand fast* therefore in the liberty wherewith Christ hath made us free, and be not entangled again with the yoke of bondage. (KJV, 2020)

Today's Devotional Topic: Stand fast, and wait on the Lord

Today's Prayer:

_____

_____

_____

_____

_____

_____

_____

_____

_____

_____

_____

_____

_____

_____

_____

_____

_____

_____

_____

_____

_____

_____

_____

_____

Prayers Answered Today:

_____

_____

_____

_____

_____

_____

_____

_____

_____

_____

_____

_____

Additional Comments:

_____

_____

_____

_____

_____

_____

Prayer Journal Day Seventy: _____

Galatians 5:1: Stand fast therefore in the liberty *wherewith Christ hath made us free, and be not entangled again with the yoke of bondage*. (KJV, 2020)

Today's Devotional Topic: Be free and not entangled with the yoke of bondage.

Today's Prayer:

_____

_____

_____

_____

_____

_____

_____

_____

_____

_____

_____

_____

_____

_____

_____

_____

_____

_____

_____

_____

_____

_____

_____

Prayers Answered Today:

_____

_____

_____

_____

_____

_____

_____

_____

_____

_____

_____

_____

Additional Comments:

_____

_____

_____

_____

_____

Prayer Journal Day Seventy-One: _____

Galatians 5:16-18: This I say then, *walk in the spirit, and ye shall not fulfill the lust of the flesh,* for the flesh lusteth against the Spirit and the spirit against the flesh: and these are contrary, the one to the other; so that ye cannot do the things that ye would. But be led of the spirit, ye are not under the law. (KJV, 2020).

Today's Devotional Topic: Walk in the spirit and not the lust of the flesh.

Today's Prayer:

_____

_____

_____

_____

_____

_____

_____

_____

_____

_____

_____

_____

_____

_____

_____

_____

_____

_____

_____

_____

_____

Prayers Answered Today:

_____

_____

_____

_____

_____

_____

_____

_____

_____

_____

_____

_____

_____

Additional Comments:

_____

_____

_____

_____

_____

Prayer Journal Day Seventy-Two: _____

Galatians 5:16-18: This I say then, walk in the spirit, and ye shall not fulfill the lust of the flesh, for the flesh lusteth against the Spirit and the spirit against the flesh: and these are contrary, the one to the other; so that ye cannot do the things that ye would. *But be led of the spirit,* ye are not under the law. (KJV, 2020).

Today's Devotional Topic: Be led by the spirit in all things

Today's Prayer:

_____

_____

_____

_____

_____

_____

_____

_____

_____

_____

_____

_____

_____

_____

_____

_____

_____

_____
_____
_____
_____
_____

Prayers Answered Today:

_____
_____
_____
_____
_____
_____
_____
_____
_____
_____
_____
_____

Additional Comments:

_____
_____
_____
_____
_____
_____

Prayer Journal Day Seventy-Three: _____

Galatians 5:19-21: The *works of the flesh* are manifest, which are these adultery, fornication, uncleanness, lasciviousness, idolatry, witchcraft, hatred, variance, wrath, emulations, strife, seditions, heresies, envying, murders, drunkenness, and reveling, and such like, of the which I tell you before, *as I have also told you in time past that they which do such things shall not inherit the kingdom of God.* (KJV, 2020).

Today's Devotional Topic: The works of the flesh shall not enter into heaven. So, they must not be in our lives!

Today's Prayer:

_____

_____

_____

_____

_____

Prayers Answered Today:

_____

_____

_____

_____

_____

_____

_____

_____

_____

_____

_____

_____

_____

Additional Comments:

_____

_____

_____

_____

Prayer Journal Day Seventy-Four: _____

Galatians 5:19-21: The *works of the flesh* are manifest, which are these *adultery*, fornication, uncleanness, lasciviousness, idolatry, witchcraft, hatred, variance, wrath, emulations, strife, seditions, heresies, envying, murders, drunkenness, and reveling, and such like, of the which I tell you before, as I have also told you in time past that they which do such things shall not inherit the kingdom of God. (KJV, 2020).

Today's Devotional Topic: Sins of the Flesh: *Adultery*

Today's Prayer:

_____

_____

_____

_____

_____

Prayers Answered Today:

_____

_____

_____

_____

_____

_____

_____

_____

_____

_____

Additional Comments:

_____

_____

_____

_____

_____

_____

Prayer Journal Day Seventy-Five: _____

Galatians 5:19-21: The *works of the flesh* are manifest, which are these adultery, *fornication,* uncleanness, lasciviousness, idolatry, witchcraft, hatred, variance, wrath, emulations, strife, seditions, heresies, envying, murders, drunkenness, and reveling, and such like, of the which I tell you before, as I have also told you in time past that they which do such things shall not inherit the kingdom of God. (KJV, 2020).

Today's Devotional Topic: Sin of the Flesh: *Fornication*

Today's Prayer:

_____

_____

_____

_____

_____

_____

_____

_____

_____

_____

_____

_____

_____

_____

_____

_____

_____
_____
_____
_____
_____

Prayers Answered Today:

_____
_____
_____
_____
_____
_____
_____
_____
_____
_____
_____
_____

Additional Comments:

_____
_____
_____
_____
_____

Prayer Journal Day Seventy-Six: _____

Galatians 5:19-21: The *works of the flesh* are manifest, which are these adultery, fornication, **uncleanness,** lasciviousness, idolatry, witchcraft, hatred, variance, wrath, emulations, strife, seditions, heresies, envying, murders, drunkenness, and reveling, and such like, of the which I tell you before, as I have also told you in time past that they which do such things shall not inherit the kingdom of God. (KJV, 2020).

Today's Devotional Topic: The Sin of Uncleanness

Today's Prayer:

_____

_____

_____

_____

_____

_____

_____

_____

_____

_____

_____

_____

_____

_____

_____

_____

_____

_____

_____

_____

_____

_____

Prayers Answered Today:

_____

_____

_____

_____

_____

_____

_____

_____

_____

_____

_____

Additional Comments:

_____

_____

_____

_____

_____

Prayer Journal Day Seventy-Seven: _____

Galatians 5:19-21: The *works of the flesh* are manifest, which are these adultery, fornication, uncleanness, *lasciviousness,* idolatry, witchcraft, hatred, variance, wrath, emulations, strife, seditions, heresies, envying, murders, drunkenness, and reveling, and such like, of the which I tell you before, as I have also told you in time past that they which do such things shall not inherit the kingdom of God. (KJV, 2020).

Today's Devotional Topic: You should not be involved in lascivious behaviors or actions, but keep your temple holy before God.

Today's Prayer:

_____

_____

_____

_____

_____

_____

_____

_____

_____

_____

_____

_____

_____

_____

_____

_____

_____

_____

_____

_____

_____

_____

Prayers Answered Today:

_____

_____

_____

_____

_____

_____

_____

_____

_____

_____

_____

_____

Additional Comments:

_____

_____

_____

_____

_____

Prayer Journal Day Seventy-Eight: _____

Galatians 5:19-21: The *works of the flesh* are manifest, which are these adultery, fornication, uncleanness, lasciviousness, *idolatry*, witchcraft, hatred, variance, wrath, emulations, strife, seditions, heresies, envying, murders, drunkenness, and reveling, and such like, of the which I tell you before, as I have also told you in time past that they which do such things shall not inherit the kingdom of God. (KJV, 2020).

Today's Devotional Topic: There are many ways to be involved in idolatry and idol worship.

Today's Prayer:

_____

_____

_____

_____

_____

_____

_____

_____

_____

_____

_____

_____

_____

_____

_____

_____

_____

_____

_____

_____

Prayers Answered Today:

_____

_____

_____

_____

_____

_____

_____

_____

_____

_____

_____

_____

_____

Additional Comments:

_____

_____

_____

_____

_____

Prayer Journal Day Seventy-Nine: _____

Galatians 5:19-21: The *works of the flesh* are manifest, which are these adultery, fornication, uncleanness, lasciviousness, idolatry, *witchcraft,* hatred, variance, wrath, emulations, strife, seditions, heresies, envying, murders, drunkenness, and reveling, and such like, of the which I tell you before, as I have also told you in time past that they which do such things shall not inherit the kingdom of God. (KJV, 2020).

Today's Devotional Topic: The lure of witchcraft and the many avenues that trap unsuspecting individuals.

Today's Prayer:

_____

_____

_____

_____

_____

_____

_____

_____

_____

_____

_____

_____

_____

_____

_____

_____

_____
_____
_____
_____
_____

Prayers Answered Today:

_____
_____
_____
_____
_____
_____
_____
_____
_____
_____
_____

Additional Comments:

_____
_____
_____
_____
_____
_____

Prayer Journal Day Eighty: _____

Galatians 5:19-21: The *works of the flesh* are manifest, which are these adultery, fornication, uncleanness, lasciviousness, idolatry, witchcraft, *hatred,* variance, wrath, emulations, strife, seditions, heresies, envying, murders, drunkenness, and reveling, and such like, of the which I tell you before, as I have also told you in time past that they which do such things shall not inherit the kingdom of God. (KJV, 2020).

Today's Devotional Topic: Hatred and its consequences

Today's Prayer:

_____
_____
_____
_____
_____

Prayers Answered Today:

_____
_____
_____
_____
_____
_____
_____
_____
_____
_____
_____
_____
_____

Additional Comments:

_____
_____
_____
_____
_____
_____

Prayer Journal Day Eighty-One: _____

Galatians 5:19-21: The *works of the flesh* are manifest, which are these adultery, fornication, uncleanness, lasciviousness, idolatry, witchcraft, hatred, *variance,* wrath, emulations, strife, seditions, heresies, envying, murders, drunkenness, and reveling, and such like, of the which I tell you before, as I have also told you in time past that they which do such things shall not inherit the kingdom of God. (KJV, 2020).

Today's Devotional Topic: The many facets of variance and why it tempts us so much!

Today's Prayer:

_____

_____

_____

_____

_____

_____

_____

_____

_____

_____

_____

_____

_____

_____

_____

_____

_____

_____

_____

Prayers Answered Today:

_____

_____

_____

_____

_____

_____

_____

_____

_____

_____

_____

Additional Comments:

_____

_____

_____

_____

_____

_____

Prayer Journal Day Eighty-Two: _____

Galatians 5:19-21: The *works of the flesh* are manifest, which are these adultery, fornication, uncleanness, lasciviousness, idolatry, witchcraft, hatred, variance, *wrath,* emulations, strife, seditions, heresies, envying, murders, drunkenness, and reveling, and such like, of the which I tell you before, as I have also told you in time past that they which do such things shall not inherit the kingdom of God. (KJV, 2020).

Today's Devotional Topic: The effects of the wrath

Today's Prayer:

_____

_____

_____

_____

_____

_____

_____

_____

_____

_____

_____

_____

_____

_____

_____

_____

_____

_____

_____

_____

_____

_____

Prayers Answered Today:

_____

_____

_____

_____

_____

_____

_____

_____

_____

_____

_____

Additional Comments:

_____

_____

_____

_____

_____

Prayer Journal Day Eighty-Three: _____

Galatians 5:19-21: The *works of the flesh* are manifest, which are these adultery, fornication, uncleanness, lasciviousness, idolatry, witchcraft, hatred, variance, wrath, *emulations,* strife, seditions, heresies, envying, murders, drunkenness, and reveling, and such like, of the which I tell you before, as I have also told you in time past that they which do such things shall not inherit the kingdom of God. (KJV, 2020).

Today's Devotional Topic: The consequences of emulations

Today's Prayer:

_____
_____
_____
_____
_____
_____
_____
_____
_____
_____
_____
_____
_____
_____
_____
_____
_____

_____

_____

_____

_____

_____

Prayers Answered Today:

_____

_____

_____

_____

_____

_____

_____

_____

_____

_____

_____

_____

_____

Additional Comments:

_____

_____

_____

_____

Prayer Journal Day Eighty-Four: _____

Galatians 5:19-21: The *works of the flesh* are manifest, which are these adultery, fornication, uncleanness, lasciviousness, idolatry, witchcraft, hatred, variance, wrath, emulations, *strife,* seditions, heresies, envying, murders, drunkenness, and reveling, and such like, of the which I tell you before, as I have also told you in time past that they which do such things shall not inherit the kingdom of God. (KJV, 2020).

Today's Devotional Topic: The bad fruit that results from strife!

Today's Prayer:

_____

_____

_____

_____

_____

Prayers Answered Today:

_____

_____

_____

_____

_____

_____

_____

_____

_____

_____

_____

_____

Additional Comments:

_____

_____

_____

_____

_____

Prayer Journal Day Eighty-Five: _____

Galatians 5:19-21: The *works of the flesh* are manifest, which are these adultery, fornication, uncleanness, lasciviousness, idolatry, witchcraft, hatred, variance, wrath, emulations, strife, ***seditions***, heresies, envying, murders, drunkenness, and reveling, and such like, of the which I tell you before, as I have also told you in time past that they which do such things shall not inherit the kingdom of God. (KJV, 2020).

Today's Devotional Topic: The bewitching spirits of sedition

Today's Prayer:

_____

Prayers Answered Today:

Additional Comments:

Prayer Journal Day Eighty-Six: _____

Galatians 5:19-21: The *works of the flesh* are manifest, which are these adultery, fornication, uncleanness, lasciviousness, idolatry, witchcraft, hatred, variance, wrath, emulations, strife, seditions, *heresies,* envying, murders, drunkenness, and reveling, and such like, of the which I tell you before, as I have also told you in time past that they which do such things shall not inherit the kingdom of God. (KJV, 2020).

Today's Devotional Topic: The devastating impact of heresies in our lives and churches.

Today's Prayer:

_____

_____

_____

_____

_____

_____

_____

_____

_____

_____

_____

_____

_____

_____

_____

_____

_____
_____
_____
_____
_____

Prayers Answered Today:

_____
_____
_____
_____
_____
_____
_____
_____
_____
_____
_____
_____

Additional Comments:

_____
_____
_____
_____
_____

Prayer Journal Day Eighty-Seven: _____

Galatians 5:19-21: The *works of the flesh* are manifest, which are these adultery, fornication, uncleanness, lasciviousness, idolatry, witchcraft, hatred, variance, wrath, emulations, strife, seditions, heresies, *envying*, murders, drunkenness, and reveling, and such like, of the which I tell you before, as I have also told you in time past that they which do such things shall not inherit the kingdom of God. (KJV, 2020).

Today's Devotional Topic: **Envying:** The silent killer in your churches

Today's Prayer:

_____

_____

_____

_____

_____

_____

_____

_____

_____

_____

_____

_____

_____

_____

_____

_____

_____

_____

_____

_____

_____

Prayers Answered Today:

_____

_____

_____

_____

_____

_____

_____

_____

_____

_____

_____

Additional Comments:

_____

_____

_____

_____

_____

Prayer Journal Day Eighty-Eight: _____

Galatians 5:19-21: The *works of the flesh* are manifest, which are these adultery, fornication, uncleanness, lasciviousness, idolatry, witchcraft, hatred, variance, wrath, emulations, strife, seditions, heresies, envying, *murders,* drunkenness, and reveling, and such like, of the which I tell you before, as I have also told you in time past that they which do such things shall not inherit the kingdom of God. (KJV, 2020).

Today's Devotional Topic: The many ways of murder.

Today's Prayer:

_____

_____

_____

_____

_____

_____

_____

_____

_____

_____

_____

_____

_____

_____

_____

_____

_____

_____

_____

_____

_____

Prayers Answered Today:

_____

_____

_____

_____

_____

_____

_____

_____

_____

_____

_____

Additional Comments:

_____

_____

_____

_____

_____

Prayer Journal Day Eighty-Nine: _____

Galatians 5:19-21: The *works of the flesh* are manifest, which are these adultery, fornication, uncleanness, lasciviousness, idolatry, witchcraft, hatred, variance, wrath, emulations, strife, seditions, heresies, envying, murders, *drunkenness,* and reveling, and such like, of the which I tell you before, as I have also told you in time past that they which do such things shall not inherit the kingdom of God. (KJV, 2020).

Today's Devotional Topic: Drunkenness and its impact on our lives.

Today's Prayer:

_____

_____

_____

_____

_____

_____

_____

_____

_____

_____

_____

_____

_____

_____

_____

_____

_____

_____

_____

_____

_____

Prayers Answered Today:

_____

_____

_____

_____

_____

_____

_____

_____

_____

_____

_____

_____

Additional Comments:

_____

_____

_____

_____

_____

_____

Prayer Journal Day Ninety: _____

Galatians 5:19-21: The *works of the flesh* are manifest, which are these adultery, fornication, uncleanness, lasciviousness, idolatry, witchcraft, hatred, variance, wrath, emulations, strife, seditions, heresies, envying, murders, drunkenness, and *reveling*, and such like, of the which I tell you before, as I have also told you in time past that they which do such things shall not inherit the kingdom of God. (KJV, 2020).

Today's Devotional Topic: Revelings and such shall not enter heaven!

Today's Prayer:

_____

_____

_____

_____

_____

Prayers Answered Today:

_____

_____

_____

_____

_____

_____

_____

_____

_____

_____

Additional Comments:

_____

_____

_____

_____

_____

_____

_____

CONCLUSION

No one is an island to himself because our choices make a
difference for generations to come!

—Anne Graham Lotz
The Daniel Key
(Lotz, 2018, p. 159)

I pray that this prayer journal has helped you to write out your request to God so that you can remain focused on God's plan and purpose for your life. You need to focus on your prayer life and remember the request that you need to bring before the Lord each day. A prayer journal is also a good praise and tracking tool. So many times, when I kneel to pray, I forget to thank God for the many things that he does for me. My prayer journal is my reminder to praise Him for the answered prayers. Re-visiting these answered prayers a few times a year also helps to keep my faith on track and a positive attitude.

We desire that you will go forth and spread the good news of the Gospel of Jesus Christ to those around you. You need to ask God to send people across your path for you to witness and help them find their purpose. As you grow spiritually, please make the following scripture your guiding principle for each day of your life and each decision you make daily. Know that God has a plan for you. It is a good plan. Just give him a chance to guide you toward that chosen path!

Jeremiah 29:11-13: For I know the thoughts that I think toward you, saith the Lord, thoughts of peace, and not of evil, to give you an expected end. Then shall ye call upon men, and ye shall go, and pray unto me, and I will hearken unto you. And ye shall see me, and find me when ye shall search for me with all of your heart. (KJV, 2020).

I want to thank you for studying and praying with us. I pray that you have enjoyed this first book, devotional, and prayer journal as much as I have enjoyed writing it! I feel that this series will change your life forever. I have designed four devotional and four prayer journals that will accompany each of these seven books. This will give you structured daily devotions for the next seven years. At the end of these seven years, you should be walking in a year of "jubilee" spiritually and financially!

Do not forget to check with your local bookstore or our website to pre-order the next devotional and prayer journal. It would be best if you did not mix any books. The HFT Publishing, Inc. online bookstore will have each book listed and the planned publication dates.

Charlie O'Neal

List of Prayer Journals

Since you have just finished reading and completing the first prayer journal for this series, I recommend checking out all four prayer journals and the matching four devotional books. These four devotional books and prayer journals correspond with the *first book* of **The Keys to Victorious Living Series**. There are seven main books with accompanying journals in this series. One book and journal will be produced each year from 2020 to 2027. There will be four devotionals with accompanying prayer journals produced for each main book to help you break down the information and study further each topic during the year. This will help you to secure a solid foundation for your spiritual life and fully comprehend the keys to victorious living as you learn daily how to successfully implement these key concepts into your life!

---

1) **"*Why am I not Living a Victorious Life*" Prayer Journal One:** This prayer journal corresponds with the first devotional book. This book contains the prayer journal pages for the first 90-days of a one-year devotional series.

   Prayer Journal Name: *Why am I not Living a Victorious Life?*
   The Keys to Victorious Living Series-Book Four
   Projected release date: March 2021

---

2) **"*Spiritual Discernment in Victorious Living*" Prayer Journal Two:** This prayer journal corresponds with the second devotional book. This book contains the prayer journal pages for the second 90-days of a one-year devotional series.

   Prayer Journal Name: *Spiritual Discernment in Victorious Living*
   The Keys to Victorious Living Series-Book Six
   Projected release date: May 2021

3) **"*Hindrances to Victorious Living*" Prayer Journal Three:** This prayer journal corresponds with the first devotional book. This book contains the prayer journal pages for the third 90-days of a one-year devotional series.

<u>**Prayer Journal Name**</u>: ***Hindrances to Victorious Living***
The Keys to Victorious Living Series-Book Eight
<u>Projected release date</u>: August 2021

4) **"*Walking in Victory*" Prayer Journal Four:** This prayer journal corresponds with the first devotional book. This book contains the prayer journal pages for the third 90-days of a one-year devotional series.

<u>**Prayer Journal Name**</u>: ***Walking in Victory***
The Keys to Victorious Living Series-Book Eight
<u>Projected release date</u>: October 2021

All prayer journals correspond with the devotional
books by the same name on the next page.

Each year there will be four devotionals and four prayer journals to accompany each of the main books listed on page 191.

List of Devotional Books

The prayer journal you just finished completing corresponds with the first devotional book in this series. All devotional books are listed below. If you have not read these books yet, we strongly encourage you to secure a copy of this book and begin this 90-day devotional journey. All four books will provide you with one year of devotions that will reinforce the keys to victorious living in your life. We promise your life will never be the same, guaranteed in Jesus' Name!

If you have not read the <u>first main book</u> **Why am I not living a Victorious Life?** (from **The Keys of Victorious Living Series),** you need to order your copy today and begin studying. The strategies discussed in these devotional books are discussed in detail in this book. (See the list of books that follows on the next couple of pages).

1) **"*Why am I not Living a Victorious Life? Devotional*" Book One:** This 90-day devotional book corresponds with the main book by the same name. This devotional has an accompanying prayer journal.

    <u>Devotional Name:</u> *Why am I not living a Victorious Life?*
    The Keys to Victorious Living Series-Book Three:
    <u>Projected release date</u>: March 2021

2) **"*Spiritual Discernment in Victorious Living Devotional*" Book Two:** This 90-day devotional book corresponds with the main book by the same name. This devotional has an accompanying prayer journal.

    <u>Devotional Name</u>: *Spiritual Discernment in Victorious Living*
    The Keys to Victorious Living Series-Book Five
    <u>Projected release date</u>: May 2021

3) **"*Hindrances to Victorious Living Devotional*" Book Three:** This 90-day devotional book corresponds with the main book by the same name. This devotional has an accompanying prayer journal.

    <u>Devotional Name:</u> *Hindrances to Victorious Living*

The Keys to Victorious Living Series-Book Seven
Projected release date: August 2021.

4) **"*Walking in Victory Devotional*" Book Four:**
This 90-day devotional book corresponds with the main book by the same name. This devotional has an accompanying prayer journal.

Devotional Name: ***Walking in Victory***
The Keys to Victorious Living Series-Book Nine
Projected release date: October 2021.

Make sure that you purchase the accompanying prayer journals for each of these devotionals. Track your prayer request, answered prayers, and offer praise to God for all that he has done for you this year!

After reading all four devotional books, you will have completed a one-year study based on *The Keys to Victorious Living.* Your life will never be the same once you put the words of life from our Lord and Savior, Jesus Christ, into your heart. You will be shocked at the changes that will manifest themselves in your life through this study of God's word.

Each year there will be four devotionals and four prayer journals to accompany each of the main books listed on page 191.

List of the Seven Main Books
in this Series

Below is a list of the books in this series. A summary of the contents of each book follows the title. We pray that these books, devotionals, and prayer journals significantly impact your life. We are praying that each person reading these books learns who you are, a Christian, God's purpose for your life, how to work toward your designed purpose, and dreams. God has given each of us a purpose. He wants to provide you with the gifts and talents needed to help you overcome opposition during a trial and secure a victorious life for you and your family.

Check online or with your local bookstore for all of these books, devotionals, and prayer journals. The anticipated release date is listed for each book. We recommend that you read each of these books in the order listed below and utilize the devotional books in your first year of study. Each book builds on the knowledge and gradually advances the reader into a lifestyle change that will result in a way to live "victorious" on your Christian walk and help others enjoy the "joy of their salvation." A full year (four 90-day devotionals) will be written that corresponds with all seven of these books. This program of books will outline your devotional studies for the next seven years. You will never be the same as you complete this journey with Charlie O'Neal, in Jesus' Name.

Main Book One:
Why am I not living a Victorious Life?
"The Keys to Victorious Living Series-Book One"

Release Date: *December 2020*

This book is the *first book* of the series on *The Keys to Victorious Living.* This book lays the foundation on which the next six books expand. You will learn how to assess your life for hindrances to living victoriously. You will receive a detailed summary of each area where work on your spiritual journey is needed. Then the next six books will provide an intensive study of each of those topics. You need to know what you believe and why. The basic concepts of living a Christian life are discussed, and the author provides you the keys to victorious living. The tools you learn to use and the knowledge obtained in this book will forever change your life. You will never look back to your old way of thinking, but you will long to move to the next book and learn more about how Christ wants us to live.

Main Book Two: *The Spiritual Warrior*
"The Keys to Victorious Living Series-Book Eleven"

Release Date: *December 2021*

In this *second main book*, (book 11 in the series), we will discuss the specifics of how to ensure that you have a solid spiritual foundation, along with a detailed study on how to be a mighty spiritual warrior in this Christian walk. Your prep and training as a spiritual warrior will determine your success with battling the principalities of darkness and maintaining a victorious Christian walk. In essence, you can be the man with the ten talents that invested wisely and had turned them into 20 talents (Victorious Living) or the man that his master gave one talent to, who buried it.

Main Book Three: *Meeting the Master*
"The Keys to Victorious Living Series-Book Twenty-One"

Release Date: *December 2022*

In this *third main book*, (book 21 in the series), we will discuss the specifics of what is required of us to meet our master and be the bride of Christ. There are special preparations that you must go through to meet the President of the United States of the King of a foreign country. You, too, must make special preparations to meet the King of Kings and Lord of Lords! You will learn how to prepare for this meeting and use your spiritual armor in this book.

Book Four: *The Pruning*
"The Keys to Victorious Living Series-Book Thirty-One"

Release Date: *December 2023*

In this *fourth main book*, (book 31 in the series), we will discuss the specifics of being groomed to meet our Lord and Savior. Just like a gardener trims back the grapevines each year to get rid of dead limbs, fungus, or disease, we will learn how God "prunes us" through his word to help us on our spiritual journey. When you finish this book, you will find that your outlook on life and trials have changed. Your focus through the trials and tests will be different as you learn to navigate spiritual warfare expertly.

Book Five: The Prayer Vat
"The Keys to Victorious Living Series-Book -Forty-One"

Release Date: *December 2024*

In this *fifth main book*, (book 41 in the series), we will discuss the specifics of daily prayer, intercessory prayer, fasting, and reading God's word. The importance of continually praying and preparing for this spiritual battle is the prep that we need for a victorious life!

Book Six: For A Time Like This!
"The Keys to Victorious Living Series-Book Fifty-One"

Release Date: *December 2025*

In this *sixth main book*, (book 51 in the series), we will discuss the specifics of why certain things will happen in our lives as God directs us toward his purpose for our lives. We will discuss how your purpose will place you in communities, churches, and your job for "a time like this," as Queen Esther and Mordechai explained in the Book of Esther. It is amazing what you learn when you begin to look at the "big picture" like God. This book will also discuss the advanced spiritual skills that you will need to live a victorious life as you move toward God's purpose for your life!

Book Seven: The Wedding Invitation
"The Keys to Victorious Living Series-Book Sixty-One"

Release Date: *December 2026*

In this *seventh main book*, (book 61 in the series), we will discuss the specifics of the Rapture and Millennial Reign. To ensure complete success and an uninhibited victorious life, you must learn the skills and keys presented in this book. As the final book in this series, the last chapters will recap the essentials from each of the seven books for a detailed review.

This series is so powerful that you will want to collect all seven main books and have them to refer back too many times in the future. You will never want to lose focus on these tools.

Do not forget that there are four devotionals and four prayer journals for each year that supports these main books, for a total of 70-books in this series that will change your life from 2020 through 2027! Join us and live a Victorious Life through the blood of Jesus Christ!

Sometimes refinement of character happens naturally as we grow older, but for many people, that growth is fostered by spiritual practices adopted and followed in a disciplined way.

—Rachel Cowan, *Wise Aging,* www.wow4u.com

References

Brainy Quotes. (2019, October 7). *Religious Quote*. (Author's names searches). Retrieved from Brainy Quotes: https://www. brainyquotes.com (then further search by name).

Dictionary.com. (2019, September 5). *Definitions* (of various words). Retrieved from Dictionary.com: https://www.dictionary. com/browse/

Google.com. (2019). *Google word and author quote searches.* All retrieved from https://www.google.com/search

KJV. (2019). *The Holy Bible-King James Version.* Retrieved from https://www.kingjamesbibleonline.org

Lotz, A. G. (2018). *The Daniel Key: 20 Choices that make all the difference.* Grand Rapids, MI: Zondervan

WOW4U.com (2019, September 5). *Spiritual quotes.* Retrieved from: www.wow4u.com

ABOUT THE AUTHOR

> *Our attitude today can determine our greatness...*
> *or our smallness...tomorrow!*
>
> —Anne Graham Lotz
> *The Daniel Key*
> (Lotz, 2018, p. 53)

The author of this prayer journal has written a seven-book series on the keys to victorious living. After positive feedback from the pre-publication reviews for the first book, Charlie O'Neal was asked by the board of directors and marketing team of Heritage House Foundation to compile four one 90-day devotional for each of the seven books. With extremely positive pre-publication feedback to the devotional, one of the local pastoral editors asked if Charlie would compile a payer journal to help young Christians get this information rooted in their minds. He was also looking for a tool to help them remain focused in their prayer lives. So, this prayer journal is a result of that pastor's request.

As you read through *The Keys to Victorious Living Series* or the *Victorious Living Devotional Series*, let God speak to your heart and journal those thoughts, prayers, and request that you make to God. Make sure that you remember to log in your answered prayers each day. At the end of these 90 days, you will be amazed at what happens when you focus your prayer life on specific goals to help you live victoriously. As you see, the prayers answered, your faith will grow to believe God for more and bigger things.

Please write to Charlie at the Heritage House Foundation offices so that the ministry will know what God has done for you. They will add you to their daily prayer list. Then they will forward your letter to Charlie to respond personally to you. Your donation or monthly partnership with **The Heritage House Foundation** will help them spread the gospel around the world. They support ministers and missionaries by helping provide housing, medical help, and food to the retired ministers and missionaries. These ministers are no longer able to preach full-time but cannot live on their social security checks. Many ministers' wives are put out of the parsonage with less than a 30-day notice (most just 2-weeks), with no concern about whether they have a place to live. This dilemma was not the intent God had for the church of today. Jesus said that we were to take care of our elders, widows, and orphans. Jesus inspired us to love our neighbor as ourselves. The scripture promises us that what we do for the man of God (or prophet of God), we will receive the prophet's reward.

Charlie O'Neal has written these seven books, the first four devotionals, and prayer journals for each devotional following a dream from God about these books. In Charlie's dream, God instructed Charlie to give 100% of the royalties to the Heritage House Foundation. All proceeds from selling these books, e-books, audiobooks, and other promotional materials will be donated to ***The Heritage House Foundation*** (HHF). HHF is a non-profit organization that will use the funds to provide housing, medical, and nutritional assistance to retired missionaries, retired ministers, and retired teachers (in churches, Bible Colleges, Christian Schools, and Missions). Other aid recipients will include ministers, pastors, key leadership staff of prison ministry outreach programs, children's homes, homes for unwed mothers, human trafficking victims' homes, and programs. The author of this book series will not receive any money or royalties from these books. All proceeds will go to ***The Heritage House Foundation***, which has been set up as an IRS 501©3 charitable organization, and IRS 509 foundation.

AUTHOR'S CREDENTIALS AND EXPERIENCE:

The author is an ordained minister, happily married, with complete spousal and family support in the ministry, missions, and other outreach programs in which they are currently involved. The author is licensed in an evangelical organization that is internationally recognized. The author has almost 30-years of ministry experience that ranges from assistant and associate pastor to senior pastor positions; international missions work in several countries, including 10/40 window countries. The author has been a keynote speaker at international conferences and all across the United States. Other exposure includes interviews and programs on several Christian networks. The author's work history includes work with several large ministries during the early years of training, in addition to having completed two master's degree programs and extensive ministry training.

MORE INFO ABOUT THIS JOURNAL SERIES:

As you read through this series of books and devotionals, focus on the content, not the author! Let God move on you how to pray. Then track your prayers and requests. You will be amazed when and how God answers them. As you follow how awesome our God is to you and your family, you will see your faith in God grow in leaps and bounds! Write to the author and Heritage House Foundation staff below. We want to hear from you and how God has impacted your life due to this book.

CONTACT INFO---HERITAGE HOUSE FOUNDATION:

This foundation is supported 100% by charitable contributions from its partners and the book royalties given to Heritage House Foundation. Contact us for information on being a monthly prayer partner, donate land and other non-monetary items. For more information on this ministry, foundation, seed faith offerings, and ministry partnership, please send your inquiries to:

Heritage House Foundation
Attention: Victorious Living Project
P. O. Box 1801
Brewton, AL 36427-1801

Email to communicate with the author: Charlie@minister.com

Email to communicate with HHF: HeritageHouse@minister.com

HERITAGE HOUSE FOUNDATION

Heritage House Foundation was initially established to provide help and assistance to missionaries returning from the mission field. When this ministry started in 1999, the founder of this foundation opened their home in Pensacola, FL, for ministers to stay with them until they could secure housing back in the states. At that time, most couples or families stayed for just a few weeks, and then their licensing organization made arrangements for housing for them.

As the economy has changed over the past couple of decades, more and more licensing agencies have deleted this post-mission assignment benefit from their services. Between 2004 and 2008, the author received numerous calls about homeless pastors' wives because their husbands had died while pastoring a church. Most of them were only give a couple of weeks up to a month to vacate the parsonage, so the church could prep and repair it for the new pastor that would be arriving. The fact that widows were being put out on the streets as homeless individuals broke this author's heart! After much prayer, the board of Heritage House Foundation decided to expand their ministry to meet these displaced individuals' needs and help them financially.

Since this new expansion was not budgeted, the foundation founder and family covered the cost of helping these widowers entirely from their personal finances, ensuring that these older adults had food and medications too. One night in 2017, God gave a dream to Charlie O'Neal that changed the focus of the Heritage House Foundation's strategic plan for 2020-2030. See *The Keys to Victorious Living Series-Book One*. *Why am I not living a Victorious Life?* This book will provide you with the purpose, mission, vision, and goals of this foundation and how Charlie's dream and donation of the royalties from this book series is helping fulfill this ministry goal. It also lists the items they need for this ministry and all contact information if you feel led to support the Heritage House Foundation each month.

HOW FUNDED:

Heritage House Foundation is funded primarily by the royalties from books that have been written by this author. Since 2009, several authors have donated royalties to this foundation. Several other non-profit organizations have given to this foundation. Heritage foundation also accepts charitable contributions from individuals. Each church that asks Heritage House to keep their guest speakers, evangelist, and missionaries for them during the year, take up at least once per year a mission offering for Heritage House's operating expenses and send it to the foundation. Some churches send monthly mission support (designated as a Home Missions outreach program by most protestant organizations). If your church or the organization that your church belongs to does not have Heritage House Foundation or Heritage House on their approved "Home Missions" list, contact us, and we will make arrangements to meet with them and go through the approval process. Note that this foundation is non-denominational. We are networked with all organizations that believe that Jesus Christ is the Son of God, born of the virgin Mary, who lived as a man, died on the cross, and rose again.

CURRENT PROJECTS:

1) **Heritage House**: Heritage House is a home that will function like a bed and breakfast half-way house for displaced ministers, missionaries, evangelists, pastors, and teachers while they are waiting to secure their homes or one to be built for them. There will be two Heritage Houses by the end of 2021 or the first part of 2022, hopefully!

2) **Oasis Estates**: A housing community of duplexes, quad-plexes, and manufactured homes, where the widowed spouses of these individuals can have low rent options for housing. This estate is especially beneficial to the spouses of ministers, missionaries, and teachers that are no longer physically able to manage a property or home. The "Heritage Village" that will be located at Oasis Estates will also have a commercial kitchen, dining room, and great room where the 30-60 residents can eat Dinner (Supper) each night and enjoy a devotion and prayer by a minister. If a resident does not want to join the group or is sick, a plate will be delivered to their apartment. This building will allow us to ensure that all of these individuals receive at least one balanced meal a day instead of cutting out food to pay for their medications.

3) **Corporate Office:**   At present, the Heritage House Foundation is working temporarily out of a manufactured home that has been converted to office space on the land that is owned by the foundation's president/CEO. There is a significant need for designated office space that is appropriate for the ministry and should be located near one of the Heritage Houses or the Village at Oasis Estates. The foundation officers are looking at a property that could be remodeled and used for the offices. At present, they have found a property that was a bed and breakfast location. It would make a perfect Heritage House and Ministry Office/Conference Center. It has an office and conference room on the main floor that would work perfectly for the foundation's office. It also has four acres of prime land in Brewton, Alabama, where the warehouse storage facilities could be built to store the donated building materials and supplies currently being given for building these homes for ministers. We are praying and believing God for the funds to secure this building and land.

4) **Heritage Village:**

At present, we have not purchased the land and homes for Heritage Village. However, there are several properties and acreage for sale in the Brewton area that would be ideal for this village's development. Heritage House Foundation board is fasting and praying for the funds to continue forward to secure this property and begin building.

There is a need for $96,000 to purchase land and $260,000 to buy property, a home, sheds, etc., on two acres of land, plus $960,000 to buy the large parcel for the village. There are an additional 200 acres in the same area (but not joining the current ministry property) that is for sale for $800,000.

We are praying over all of these properties, asking God to direct us to which properties to buy and the money needed to purchase the land and develop it for additional housing. If we could obtain these parcels of land and create the two Heritage Villages, the impact would be significant locally and for ministers and missionaries returning to the United States to live. We want a Village where ministerial couples can still take care of themselves without any assistance needed except financial and housing. There is a long-term plan for a village that would provide widowed ministers in addition to housing, financial, housekeeping, and dietary assistance. Note that these two villages would not provide Assisted Living (ALF) or Nursing Home/Rehab services.

ITEMS CURRENTLY NEEDED:

1) All types of building supplies, lumber, and various materials for completing the inside of homes. Materials required for new construction and remodeling.

2) All types of construction equipment (hand tools).

3) Bulldozer, back-hoe, and ditch witch.

4) Flatbed trailers to haul this equipment.

5) Dual-axel (large engine) crew-cab truck to pull the flatbed

6) All types of appliances for the homes being build or remodeled. The appliances needed include but are not limited to stoves, ovens, refrigerators, microwaves, ice makers (under-counter), built-in dishwashers, washers, dryers, and water heaters, etc. Used appliances are accepted as long as they are working correctly and in good condition. We do not have anyone to repair them.

7) Vehicles (used and new cars, trucks, and golf carts) that can be utilized by the individuals we are building these homes for; they are returning from the mission field with nothing).

8) All types of kitchen utensils, dishes, glasses, and cookware (new only).

9) All types of small kitchen appliances (mixers, bread makers, can openers, hot pots, hot plates, grills, smokers, coffee pots, grinders, blenders, electric fryers, canners, crock-pots, electric cookers, etc.).

10) King and Queen size bedding (sheets, spreads, comforters, etc.). Only new items.

11) Curtains, blinds, shades, and other window treatments. (Only new items).

12) Interior design items. Includes flooring, wallpaper, lights, lamps, and furniture. (Used in good condition and new accepted).

13) Ready to assemble kitchen cabinets, countertops (all types of granite, marble, quartz, quartzite, chorion, ceramic tile, and Formica.

14) Tubs, shower stalls, tub enclosures, sinks, bathroom cabinets, soaking tubs, etc.

15) Door units (exterior and interior units).

16) Porch rocking chairs

17) Porch tables and chair

18) Patio tables and chairs

19) Light fixtures, ceiling fans, lamps, and electrical supplies.

20) Plumbing supplies, fixtures, sinks, toilets, bathroom décor accessories

21) RVs and trucks to pull them around. These will be used for temporary housing while the houses are being built.

22) Closed-in utility trailers, cars, trucks, and equipment haulers for moving the needed supplies and repair supplies.

23) All types of paint supplies, stains, and paint.

24) We desperately need a wheelchair van and a transport van for each property location.
25) We need 12 fully functional golf carts at this time. More will be required as we expand the properties.
26) We need three John Deere Gators (other brands would work too). Four-wheelers with hitches and cargo trailers/haulers designed for pulling with a Gator or four-wheeler is needed.
27) Five riding lawn mowers, preferably zero-turn units, are needed.

<u>Authors currently contribute 100% of their royalties for the Christian Books that they have written to this foundation.</u>

1) Charlie O'Neal (donating a 70-book series over seven years).
2) Charles Edward Nall (first book coming out in Fall 2021).
3) La Wanda Blackmon (She is donating four devotional books and four prayer journals. The first one is scheduled for release in Spring 2021).

If you would like to join this list of authors and donate your royalties from a book, you have written, or that you are currently writing, please contact the Heritage House Foundation at the address below. A contract and forms will be sent to you for completion. If you are starting as a writer, donate your royalties and watch as God promotes your book and makes you a household name for his honor and glory. You will find as these authors above that you cannot out-give God!

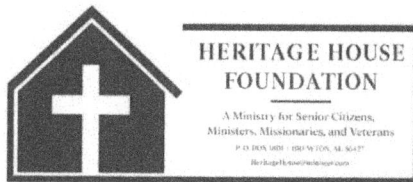

HERITAGE HOUSE FOUNDATION
A Ministry for Senior Citizens, Ministers, Missionaries, and Veterans
P O BOX 1801 · BREWTON, AL 36427
HeritageHouse@minister.com

Heritage House Foundation
P O Box 1801
Brewton, AL 36427
HeritageHouse@minister.com